大舞（中英双语）

Dawu (Chinese-English)

孙佐枫 著
林记明 译

中国传统文化『走出去』丛书之二

Chinese Traditional Culture "Going Out" Series II

林记明 孙佐枫 丛书主编

河北出版传媒集团
河北人民出版社
石家庄

图书在版编目（CIP）数据

大舞 : 汉、英 / 孙佐枫著 ; 林记明译. -- 石家庄: 河北人民出版社, 2022.12
（中国传统文化“走出去”丛书 ; 之二）
ISBN 978-7-202-16222-4

Ⅰ. ①大… Ⅱ. ①孙… ②林… Ⅲ. ①健身运动—基本知识—中国—汉、英 Ⅳ. ①G883

中国版本图书馆CIP数据核字(2022)第248752号

丛 书 名 中国传统文化“走出去”丛书之二
ZHONGGUO CHUANTONG WENHUA ZOUCHUQU CONGSHU ZHIER
丛书主编 林记明 孙佐枫
书 名 大舞（汉英双语）
DAWU HANYING SHUANGYU
著 者 孙佐枫
译 者 林记明

总 策 划 王斌贤
策划编辑 路殿国 李成轩
责任编辑 赵 蕊
美术编辑 王 婧
责任校对 余尚敏
摄 影 蔡欣然

出版发行 河北出版传媒集团 河北人民出版社
（石家庄市友谊北大街 330 号）
印 刷 河北新华第一印刷有限责任公司
开 本 787 毫米×1092 毫米 1/16
印 张 5.25
字 数 68 000
版 次 2022 年 12 月第 1 版 2022 年 12 月第 1 次印刷
书 号 ISBN 978-7-202-16222-4
定 价 25.00 元

<<<前言 Foreword

大舞是以古代朴实的舞蹈动作为基础，融合传统导引的“三调”来宣发、疏通、调节人体气机，改善气血运行。以舞宣导，通利关节；以神领舞，以舞练形；外动内舞，意气相随来表现其功法特点。其集历史功法之精华，融入现代相关学科理论，是集体智慧的结晶，充分体现了科学性；以中医、现代体育以及相关科学理论为基础，功理和功效一并考量，具有明显的健身性。本书中英对照，从功法操作、学练要领、功理作用、适宜症状等方面进行通俗易懂的论述。长期坚持练习本功法，可改善人体的肩、颈和腰椎关节不适，预防跌倒摔跤，提高人体平衡能力，对心血管、高血压、糖尿病、肺病、抑郁症等均有不同程度的改善效果。因此，非常适宜在中外健身人群中普及推广。在倡导文化自信、建设文化强国和健康中国的时代背景下，本书在中国传统文化的国际传播方面具有文化和健身价值。

Dawu incorporates the “three regulations” of traditional *Daoyin* into ancient dance movements to dredge meridians, ventilate and regulate *Qi* in human body for the improvement of *Qi* and blood circulation. It takes dance movements to exercise and ease the joints. In the practice, the mind guides the movements, which train the body. “External movements” and “internal dance” , with intention and *Qi* in harmony, are its characteristics. Dawu combines the essence of ancient exercises and modern theories of related disciplines. Therefore, it is the crystallization of collective wisdom. Based on the traditional Chinese medicine, modern sports and related scientific theories, Dawu takes its principles and efficacy into account, with obvious fitness effects. This book in Chinese and English contains instructions, key points, functions and effects, and indications, which are easy to understand. Long-term practice of this exercise can improve the discomfort of shoulders, neck and lumbar joints, the balance of human body, cardiovascular diseases, hypertension, diabetes, pulmonary diseases, depression, and prevent falls. Therefore, it is very suitable for Chinese and foreign fitness people. In the context of advocating cultural confidence and building a strong cultural and healthy China, this book has cultural and fitness values in the international dissemination of traditional Chinese culture.

<<< 目录

Contents

预备势 / 001
Preparation / 001

第一式　昂首势 / 004
Posture 1　Hold Head High / 004

第二式　开胯势 / 008
Posture 2　Open Hips / 008

第三式　抻腰势 / 017
Posture 3　Extend Waist / 017

第四式　震体势 / 025
Posture 4　Shake Body / 025

第五式　揉脊势 / 036
Posture 5　Rub Spine / 036

第六式　摆臀势 / 043
Posture 6　Swing Hips / 043

第七式　摩肋势 / 052
Posture 7　Massage Ribs / 052

第八式　飞身势 / 062
Posture 8　Flying Stance / 062

收势 / 072
Closing / 072

预备势

Preparation

一、功法操作

I. Instructions

动作一：两脚并拢，自然站立；两肩松展，两臂自然垂于体侧；目视前下方。（图 1）

Movement 1: Stand naturally with your feet together. With the shoulders relaxed and stretching, your two arms hang naturally on both sides of the body. Eyes look down to the front. (Figure 1)

动作二：两掌缓缓上托，指尖相对，掌心向上，经腹前至膈肌同高；目视前下方。（图 2）

Movement 2: Hold your hands up slowly to the height of your diaphragm, palms up, with your fingers pointing to each other. Eyes look down to the front. (Figure 2)

图 1/Figure 1

图 2/Figure 2

动作三：两小臂外展与肩等宽；两掌指尖向前、向两侧外旋至掌心斜向上。（图 3）

Movement 3: Extend your forearms outward, shoulder width apart. Turn the fingers of both palms forward and outward to both sides until the palms are obliquely upward. (Figure 3)

动作四：两臂上举至额部前上方，两手臂夹角约 90°，掌心斜相对；配合吸气，动作略停；目视前上方。（图 4）

Movement 4: Lift your arms up to the upper front of your forehead, with a 90° angle between your arms, palms obliquely facing each other. Inhale. Make a small pause. Eyes look to the upper front. (Figure 4)

动作五：沉肩垂肘，两臂内收，两手至胸前十指相对，继续下按与肚脐同高，掌心向下，两掌相距约 10 厘米；同时，屈膝下蹲约 45°；配合呼气；目视前下方。（图 5）

Movement 5: With your shoulders sinking and your elbows dropping, withdraw your arms inward to your chest, fingers pointing to each other. Continue to press your hands down to navel height, palms down, about 10cm apart. At the same time, bend your knees to about 45°. Exhale. Eyes look down to the front. (Figure 5)

图 3/Figure 3

图 4/Figure 4

图 5/Figure 5

二、学练要领

II. Key Points

1. 并步站立时，百会穴虚领，下颏微收，松肩垂肘，两掌心轻贴大腿外侧。周身中正。

When standing with your feet together, keep your body upright, with *Baihui* acupoint gently pulled up and your chin slightly inward. Relax your shoulders and sink your elbows, with your palms lightly touching the outer thighs.

2. 唇齿合拢，自然呼吸，面带微笑。

Close your lips and teeth. Breathe naturally with a smile.

3. 两臂上举时眼神引领着手臂向头前上方伸展。

When you lift your arms, your eyes lead them to extend to the upper front of your head.

三、功理功用

III. Functions and Effects

气沉丹田，体松心静，为练功做好准备。

Relax and be calm. Sink *Qi* to the *Dantian*. Get ready for the exercise.

四、适宜症状

IV. Indications

可以缓解和改善精神紧张、焦虑、神经衰弱等相关症状。

It can relieve and improve mental stress, anxiety and neurasthenia.

第一式 昂首势

Posture 1 Hold Head High

一、功法操作

I. Instructions

动作一：左脚向左开步自然站立，两脚间距略宽于肩，脚尖向前；两臂侧起，自然伸展，掌心向上；配合吸气；目视前方。（图 6）

Movement 1: Step your left foot to the left, with the distance between feet slightly wider than shoulder width. Stand naturally, toes forward. Both of your arms rise from the sides and stretch naturally, palms up. Inhale. Eyes look ahead. (Figure 6)

动作二：屈膝下蹲，大腿和小腿夹角约 45°；抬头翘尾，脊柱反弓，沉肩曲肘，掌心向上，压腕上托约与耳高，大小臂夹角约 90°，指尖向外；配合吸气；抬头目视前上方。（图 7）

图 6/Figure 6

图 7/Figure 7

Movement 2: Bend your knees at an angle of about 45° between your thigh and calf. Raise your head and tailbone, and bend your spine back. With your shoulders sinking and elbows dropping, palms up, lift your hands up to the height of your ears, fingers pointing outward, wrists pressed. The angle between the arms is about 90°. Inhale. Eyes look up to the front. (Figure 7)

动作三：两腿自然站立，同时头正尾垂，两臂外展；配合吸气；目视前方。（图 8）

Movement 3: Straighten your legs naturally, with your head upright and tailbone dropping down. Stretch your arms outward. Exhale. Eyes look ahead. (Figure 8)

动作四：左腿收回并步站立；同时两手上抱指尖相对，配合吸气；目视前方。（图 9）

Movement 4: Bring your left leg back and stand with your feet together. At the same time, hold your hands up, fingers pointing to each other. Inhale. Eyes look ahead. (Figure 9)

图 8/Figure 8

图 9/Figure 9

动作五：沉肩垂肘两臂内收，两手至胸前十指相对，继续下按与肚脐同高，掌心向下，两手指尖相距约 10 厘米；两掌距肚脐约 10 厘米；同时，屈膝下蹲约 45°；配合呼气；目视前下方。（图 10）

Movement 5: With your shoulders sinking and elbows dropping, press your hands down to your chest, palms down, fingers pointing to each other, and further down to your navel height, about 10cm apart. The palms are about 10cm away from the navel. At the same time, bend your knees at about 45°. Exhale. Eyes look down to the front. (Figure 10)

图 10/Figure 10

右式动作同左式，动作相同，唯左右相反。一左一右各做一遍。

Repeat Movements 1 to 5, but only with left and right reversed.

二、学练要领

II. Key Points

1. 左脚开步时，两腿自然站立和两臂侧平举同时完成，上下相随。

When stepping your left foot to the left, stand naturally and raise your arms from the sides at the same time.

2. 抬头翘尾时以神道穴为中心，肩胛骨适度挤压内收。头正尾垂放松时，先松开肩胛骨再放松头尾；两掌上托时，腕关节要充分屈伸。

When raising head and tailbone, moderately squeeze and retract your shoulder blades toward *Shendao* acupoint. Relax your shoulder blades before holding head upright and dropping tailbone down. When lifting hands up, flex and stretch your wrist joints fully.

3. 两臂内收下按时，沿肩垂肘，胸、腰、胯、膝依次放松，节节贯穿，气沉丹田。

When pressing hands down, sink your shoulders and elbows. Relax your chest, waist, hips and knees in sequence.Sink *Qi* to the *Dantian*.

三、功理功用

III. Functions and Effects

1. 壮阳益气，宁心安神。

It helps to invigorate *Yang*, replenish *Qi*, and tranquilize the mind.

2. 调理心肺功能，改善胸腹血液分布。

It helps to regulate cardiopulmonary function and improve blood distribution in chest and abdomen.

3. 脊柱反弓可有效牵引椎间关节。

Bending the spine back helps stretch intervertebral joints effectively.

四、适宜症状

IV. Indications

可以缓解和改善心痛、失眠健忘、颈肩背痛、咳嗽、气喘、过敏性皮炎等相关症状。

It can relieve and improve heartache, insomnia, forgetfulness, neck and shoulder pain, cough, asthma and allergic dermatitis.

第二式　开胯势

Posture 2　Open Hips

一、功法操作

I. Instructions

动作一：重心右移，提左膝向左前方上步成左弓步，两臂侧起向前划弧，掌心相对至头顶前上方，两掌相距约 20 厘米，配合吸气，目视前上方。（图 11）

Movement 1: With the weight shifting to the right, lift the left knee and step forward to the left into a left-weighted bow stance. Arc your arms up and forward from the sides to the upper front of the head, palms facing each other, about 20cm apart. Inhale. Eyes look to the upper front. (Figure 11)

动作二：右脚上步至左脚内侧，右脚掌着地成右丁步，两膝微屈；同时两手回收至额前，与额相距约 5 厘米；目视前方。（图

图 11/Figure 11

图 12/Figure 12

12）

Movement 2: Bring your right foot to the inside of your left foot, the ball of your right foot on the ground, a T-shaped stance formed. Both knees are slightly bent. At the same time, bring your hands to about 5cm away from the forehead. Eyes look ahead. (Figure 12)

动作三：屈膝下蹲，大小腿夹角约 45°；臀部向左摆，右脚以脚掌为轴蹍转，右膝外展开胯；同时两臂向两侧分掌外展，左掌与肩同高，掌心向右上方，指尖向左上方，肘微屈，手臂成弧形，右掌至右上方约 45°，成弧形，掌心斜向玉枕穴，指尖向上；配合呼气，动作略停，目视左手。（图 13 正面、图 13 背面）

Movement 3: Bend your knees, with the angle between the thigh and calf about 45°. With your hips swinging to the left and right foot turning around the ball of your foot, turn your right knee outward to open hips. At the same time, spread your arms outward to both sides, with the left palm to shoulder level, facing up to the right, fingers pointing up to the left, and the right palm to the upper right at a 45° angle, facing *Yuzhen* acupoint, fingers pointing up. Both arms are slightly bent in an arc shape. Exhale. Make a small pause. Eyes look at your left hand. (Figure 13 front, Figure 13 back)

图 13 正面 /Figure 13 front

图 13 背面 /Figure 13 back

动作四：右脚掌踝转至脚尖向前，两腿自然站立，两臂外展成侧平举。（图 14）

Movement 4: With the ball of your right foot turning until your toes point forward, stand naturally, and extend your arms horizontally. (Figure 14)

动作五：同动作一，唯左右相反。（图 15）

Movement 5: Repeat Movement 1, but with left and right reversed. (Figure 15)

动作六：同动作二，唯左右相反。（图 16）

Movement 6: Repeat Movement 2, but with left and right reversed. (Figure 16)

图 14/Figure 14

图 15/Figure 15

图 16/Figure 16

动作七：同动作三，唯左右相反。（图 17 正面、图 17 背面）

Movement 7: Repeat Movement 3, but with left and right reversed. (Figure 17 front, Figure 17 back)

动作八：同动作四，唯左右相反。（图 18）

Movement 8: Repeat Movement 4, but with left and right reversed. (Figure 18)

动作九：左脚向左后方退步成右弓步，两臂向前划弧，掌心

相对至头顶前上方，两掌相距约 20 厘米，配合吸气，目视前上方。（图 19）

Movement 9: Step your left foot back to the left into a right-weighted bow stance. Arc your arms forward to the upper front of your head, palms facing each other, about 20cm apart. Inhale. Eyes look to the upper front. (Figure 19)

图 17 正面 /Figure 17 front

图 17 背面 /Figure 17 back

图 18/Figure 18

图 19/Figure 19

动作十：右脚退步至左脚内侧，右脚掌着地成右丁步，两膝微屈；同时两手回收至额前，与额相距约 5 厘米；目视前方。（图 20）

Movement 10: Step your right foot back to the inside of your left foot, with the ball of your right foot on the ground, a T-shaped stance formed. Both knees are slightly bent. At the same time, bring your hands to about 5cm away from the forehead. Eyes look ahead. (Figure 20)

动作十一：同动作三。（图 21）

Movement 11: Repeat Movement 3. (Figure 21)

图 20/Figure 20

图 21/Figure 21

动作十二：同动作四。（图 22）

Movement 12: Repeat Movement 4. (Figure 22)

动作十三：同动作九，唯左右相反。（图 23）

Movement 13: Repeat Movement 9, but with left and right reversed. (Figure 23)

动作十四：同动作十，唯左右相反。（图 24）

Movement 14: Repeat Movement 10, but with left and right reversed. (Figure 24)

动作十五：同动作三，唯左右相反。（图 25）

Movement 15: Repeat Movement 3, but with left and right reversed. (Figure 25)

图 22/Figure 22

图 23/Figurc 23

图 24/Figure 24

图 25/Figure 25

动作十六：同动作四，唯左右相反。（图 26）

Movement 16: Repeat Movement 4, but with left and right reversed. (Figure 26)

动作十七：两手上抱指尖相对，配合吸气；目视前方。（图 27）

Movement 17: Hold your hands up, fingers pointing to each other. Inhale. Eyes look ahead. (Figure 27)

图 26/Figure 26

图 27/Figure 27

动作十八：沉肩垂肘两臂内收，两手至胸前十指相对，继续下按与肚脐同高，掌心向下，两手指尖相距约 10 厘米；两掌距肚脐约 10 厘米；同时，屈膝下蹲，大小腿夹角约 45°；配合呼气；目视前下方。（图 28）

图 28/Figure 28

Movement 18: With your shoulders sinking and elbows dropping, press your hands down to your chest, palms down, fingers pointing to each other, and further down to your navel height, about 10cm apart. The palms are about 10cm away from the navel. At the same time, bend your knees at about 45°. Exhale. Eyes look down to the front. (Figure 28)

右式动作同左式，动作相同，唯左右相反。前进两步后退两步，一左一右各做两遍。

Repeat the movements to the left, but in the opposite direction. Take two steps forward and two steps back. Do the movements twice on either side.

二、学练要领

II. Key Points

1. 转头时要立项竖脊，左右平转。

Turn your head horizontally to the right or left, with your neck and back upright.

2. 两臂左右分掌时，肩胛骨放松，充分外展。

When separating your arms from each other, relax and extend the shoulder blades fully.

3. 两掌收回时，劳宫穴与印堂穴同高。

Bring your hands back, with *Laogong* acupoints at *Yintang* acupoint level.

4. 摆臀要充分，两肋部带动尾椎、腰椎、颈椎逐节拔伸。

Swing the hips fully so that the ribs drive the caudal vertebra, lumbar vertebra and cervical vertebra to stretch out one by one.

5. 上步、退步时动作重心要平稳，速度要均匀。

When stepping forward or backward, stabilize the weight with even speed.

三、功理功用

III. Functions and Effects

1. 以舞宣导，疏肝理气，开胯展臂，肝气生发。

It takes dance movements to soothe the liver, invigorate liver *Qi*, open the hips, and extend arms.

2. 通利关节以除寒湿，固本宣肺，排毒返清，身心安康。

It helps ease the joints to remove cold and dampness, strengthen the body constitution, disperse lung *Qi*, detoxicate, clear away heat, and improve physical and mental health.

3. 增强下肢力量，提高平衡能力。

It helps strengthen lower limbs and improve the balance.

四、适宜症状

IV. Indications

可以改善身体乏力，精神烦躁；消化系统功能紊乱；平衡感差，肢体不协调等症状。

It can improve physical fatigue, mental irritability, digestive system dysfunction, poor sense of balance, and limb disharmony.

第三式　抻腰势

Posture 3　Extend Waist

一、功法操作

I. Instructions

动作一：右脚内扣，左脚以脚跟为轴脚尖外展，身体左转约90°；同时两手在胸前合掌，与胸相距约10厘米，指尖向前上方；目视前方。（图29）

Movement 1: Turn your right foot inward. With the heel pivoting, turn your left foot outward, your body turning to the left by about 90°. At the same time, put your hands together in front, about 10cm away from your chest, fingertips pointing up to the front. Eyes look ahead. (Figure 29)

动作二：右腿自然站立，左膝提起，脚尖自然下垂，上体姿势保持不变。（图30）

图 29/Figure 29

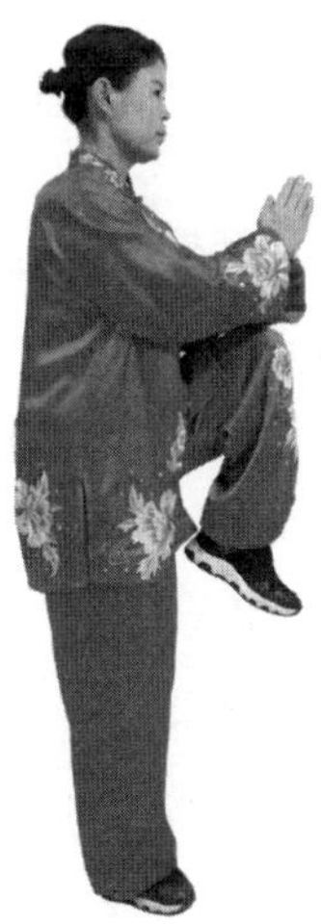

图 30/Figure 30

Movement 2: Stand naturally with your right leg. Lift your left knee, toes drooping. Keep your upper body unchanged. (Figure 30)

动作三：左脚脚尖勾起，脚跟向前蹬出，左腿伸直；目视前方。（图 31）

Movement 3: Kick forward with your left heel, ankle flexed, and straighten your left leg. Eyes look ahead. (Figure 31)

动作四：左脚落地，成左弓步，目视前方。（图 32）

Movement 4: Land with your left foot into a left-weighted bow stance. Eyes look ahead. (Figure 32)

图 31/Figure 31

图 32/Figure 32

动作五：两脚不动身体前倾约 45°；同时两掌向前上方伸展至两臂贴耳；先目视前上方，随着两臂内侧贴耳同时缓缓收下颏，再目视前下方。（图 33）

Movement 5: With your feet planted on the ground, lean forward about 45°. At the same time, extend your two palms up to the front, arms against the ears. Look up to the front first, and tuck your chin in slowly as your arms touch your ears, and then look down to the front. (Figure 33)

动作六：左脚不动，右脚跟离地，脚趾抓地。同时手臂持续

向前上方引伸，配合吸气；动作略停，目视前下方。（图 34）

Movement 6: With your left foot remaining in place, lift your right heel off, toes grasping the ground. At the same time, extend your arms further up to the front. Exhale. Make a small pause. Eyes look down to the front. (Figure 34)

图 33/Figure 33

图 34/Figure 34

动作七：重心后坐，右脚跟落地，屈膝，左腿伸直，勾脚尖。同时抬头、挺胸、塌腰、翘臀，成反背弓；两手合掌收回，约与胸同高，指尖向前上方；目视前上方。（图 35）

图 35/Figure 35

Movement 7: With your weight shifting backward, land with your right heel, knees bent. Straighten your left leg, toes turned up. At the same time, raise your head, chest out, waist down, and hips up, to form a reverse back bow. Bring your joined palms back, about the same height as your chest, fingers pointing up to the front. Eyes look up to the front. (Figure 35)

动作八至动作十三：同动作二至动作七，动作重复一遍，接做动作十四。

Movements 8 to 13: Repeat Movements 2 to 7. Then come to Movement 14.

动作十四：起身，左脚掌内扣约 135°，右脚尖外展约 135°；同时身体右转 180°；目视前方。（图 36）

Movement 14: Pull yourself up. Turn your left foot inward about 135°, and your right foot outward about 135°, your body turning 180° to the right. Eyes look ahead. (Figure 36)

动作十五：同动作二，唯左右相反。（图 37）

Movement 15: Repeat Movement 2, but only with left and right reversed. (Figure 37)

图 36/Figure 36

图 37/Figure 37

动作十六：同动作三，唯左右相反。（图 38）

Movement 16: Repeat Movement 3, but only with left and right reversed. (Figure 38)

动作十七：同动作四，唯左右相反。（图 39）

Movement 17: Repeat Movement 4, but only with left and right reversed. (Figure 39)

动作十八：同动作五，唯左右相反。（图 40）

Movement 18: Repeat Movement 5, but only with left and right reversed. (Figure 40)

动作十九：同动作六，唯左右相反。（图 41）

Movement 19: Repeat Movement 6, but only with left and right reversed. (Figure 41)

图 38/Figure 38

图 39/Figure 39

图 40/Figure 40

图 41/Figure 41

动作二十：同动作七，唯左右相反。（图 42）

Movement 20: Repeat Movement 7, but only with left and right reversed. (Figure 42)

动作二十一：起身，右脚尖内扣 90°，左脚跟蹍转，两脚尖方向正向前；自然站立，目视前方。（图 43）

Movement 21: Pull yourself up. Turn your right toes inward about 90°, and your left toes outward with the heel pivoting, to stand naturally with the toes of your feet pointing forward. Eyes look ahead. (Figure 43)

动作二十二：屈膝下蹲约 45° ；同时两掌跟分开，指尖相对，掌心向下，按至与肚脐同高；目视前下方。（图 44）

Movement 22: Bend your knees about 45°. At the same time, with the bases of palms being separated, fingers pointing to each other, press your palms down to the height of your navel, facing down. Eyes look down to the front. (Figure 44)

图 42/Figure 42

图 43/Figure 43

图 44/Figure 44

二、学练要领

II. Key Points

1. 上步时，要避免两脚前后在一条直线上，保持身体重心平稳。

When stepping forward, keep your weight stable to avoid placing your feet in a straight line.

2. 两手合掌向前上方引伸时，手臂、躯干、后腿和脚成一条直线，节节带动，两头牵引，中间放松，对拉拔长。

When your joined palms extend up to the front, your arms, torso, hind leg and feet should form a straight line, driven by the hands and feet, with the waist relaxed.

3. 合掌时，掌跟桡侧与膻中穴相距约 15 厘米，两掌之间成空心。

When you put your palms together, the radial sides of palms are about 15cm away from *Danzhong* acupoint, with a hollow between them.

4. 转身时，内扣脚要充分，注意膝关节跟脚尖在同一方向。

When turning your body, turn your foot inward as much as possible. Make sure that your knee is in the same direction of your foot.

三、功理功用

III. Functions and Effects

1. 手脚两头牵引，抻筋拔骨，通经活络，调理三焦。

With your hands extending and toes grasping the ground, tendons and bones are stretched, meridians are dredged, and collaterals are activated so that the triple energizer is regulated.

2. 后坐抬头翘尾，脊柱反弓可调理任督二脉和心肺功能，对颈椎、腰椎和下肢关节有保健和康复作用。

With your weight shifting backward, raising the head and tailbone, and bending the spine back can regulate the circulation along conception and governor meridians and the cardiopulmonary function. It has health care and rehabilitation effects on cervical vertebra, lumbar vertebra and lower limb joints.

四、适宜症状

IV. Indications

有助于疏松颈部和背部的肌肉粘连，缓解肩、肘、腕、颈、背、腰等部位的疼痛。

It can help to loosen the muscle adhesion of neck and back, and relieve the pain of shoulder, elbow, wrist, neck, back or waist.

第四式　震体势

Posture 4　Shake Body

一、功法操作

I. Instructions

动作一：两腿自然站立；同时两臂侧起成侧平举；配合吸气；目视前方。（图 45）

Movement 1: Straighten your legs naturally. At the same time, lift your arms laterally at shoulder level. Inhale. Eyes look ahead. (Figure 45)

动作二：屈膝下蹲成半马步；同时两臂从体侧下落至与肚脐同高，屈肘内收，约与肩宽，掌心向上，指尖向前；配合呼气；目视掌心。（图 46）

Movement 2: Bend your knees into a semi-horse-riding stance. At the same time, drop your arms from the sides of the body to about

图 45/Figure 45

图 46/Figure 46

navel height, with the elbows bent, about shoulder width, palms up, fingers pointing forward. Exhale. Eyes look at the palms. (Figure 46)

动作三：两腿自然站立，同时两手握固，拇指指尖放在无名指指根处，随后从小指到食指依次握固，拳心向上，拳轮轻贴肚脐两侧；目视前方。（图 47）

Movement 3: Straighten your legs naturally. At the same time, clench your fists firmly, with the tips of your thumbs put on the bases of your ring fingers, and then little fingers, ring fingers, middle fingers and index fingers doubled firmly in turn, hearts of your fists up and fifth-finger sides of your fists lightly touching the sides of your navel. Eyes look ahead. (Figure 47)

动作四：重心右移提左膝，左脚尖勾起；同时，两拳内旋上提，拳面经耳门提至头上方，拳面相对，相距约 10 厘米；配合吸气；目视前方。（图 48）

Movement 4: With the weight shifting to the right, lift the left knee, toes up. At the same time, rotating inward, your fists rise by ears, pausing over your head, fist faces opposite to each other, about 10cm apart. Inhale. Eyes look ahead. (Figure 48)

图 47/Figure 47

图 48/Figure 48

动作五：左腿放松下落，脚不触地，左脚掌落于右脚弓旁；同时，两拳慢慢变掌从两侧内旋下落，并用手背拇指侧轻敲大腿外侧中线处；配合呼气；目视前方。（图 49）

Movement 5: Relax your left leg and drop it down, the ball of your left foot beside the arch of your right. At the same time, slowly opening into palms, your hands rotate inward to drop down from both sides, and tap the midlines of your outer thighs with the thumb sides of hand backs. Exhale. Eyes look ahead. (Figure 49)

动作六：左脚向左开步，稍宽于肩，两腿自然站立；同时，两臂顺势侧起，臂与身体夹角约 45°。（图 50）

Movement 6: Step to the left with your left foot, slightly wider than shoulder width. Stand naturally. At the same time, raise your arms from both sides, the angle between the arms and the body about 45°. (Figure 50)

图 49/Figure 49

图 50/Figure 50

动作七：两脚不动，抡臂，以腰带臂，左手外旋弧形摆至体前正中线，约与胸高，掌心向上握固；同时，带动右手内旋弧形摆至体后正中线，约与腰同高，掌心向上；配合吸气；目视左手。（图 51 正面、图 51 侧面）

Movement 7: With your feet unmoved, swing your arms, waist as the driving force. As your left hand rotates outward in an arc to the midline in front of your body, about chest height, clench it tightly, palm up. At the same time, your right hand rotates inward in an arc to the midline behind the body, about waist height, palm up. Inhale. Eyes look at your left hand. (Figure 51 front, Figure 51 side)

图 51 正面 /Figure 51 front

图 51 侧面 /Figure 51 side

动作八：两腿微屈膝；同时，身体转正，左拳拳轮轻击下腹部，右拳拳眼轻击骶骨；配合吸气；目视前下方。（图 52 正面、图 52 背面）

Movement 8: As your knees bend slightly, turn your body back to the front. Tap the lower abdomen with the fifth finger side of your left fist, and the sacrum with the thumb side of your right fist. Inhale. Eyes look down to the front. (Figure 52 front, Figure 52 back)

动作九：两腿自然伸直；同时，躯干右转 90°，两拳变掌，左掌向右穿出，掌心向上，与胸同高，右掌向左穿出，掌心斜向上，与腰同高；目视右手。（图 53）

Movement 9: Straighten your legs naturally. At the same time, turn your torso 90° to the right. With the fists opening into palms, the left one pierces out to the right, facing up, about chest height, and the right one to the left, facing diagonally up, about waist height. Eyes look at the right hand. (Figure 53)

动作十：左转腰，以腰带臂，左臂从体前，右臂从体后，弧形摆至侧平举；目视前方。（图 54）

Movement 10: Turn your waist to the left. With the waist as the driving force, your left arm from the front of the body and your right arm from the back of the body swing in an arc to the sides at shoulder level. Eyes look ahead. (Figure 54)

图 52 正面 /Figure 52 front

图 52 背面 /Figure 52 back

图 53/Figure 53

图 54/Figure 54

动作十一：同动作二。（图 55）

Movement 11: Repeat Movement 2. (Figure 55)

动作十二：同动作三。（图 56）

Movement 12: Repeat Movement 3. (Figure 56)

动作十三：同动作四，唯左右相反。（图 57）

Movement 13: Repeat Movement 4, but only with left and right reversed. (Figure 57)

图 55/Figure 55

图 56/Figure 56

图 57/Figure 57

动作十四：同动作五，唯左右相反。（图 58）

Movement 14: Repeat Movement 5, but only with left and right reversed. (Figure 58)

动作十五：同动作六，唯左右相反。（图 59）

Movement 15: Repeat Movement 6, but only with left and right reversed. (Figure 59)

动作十六：同动作七，唯左右相反。（图 60 正面、图 60 侧面）

Movement 16: Repeat Movement 7, but only with left and right reversed. (Figure 60 front, Figure 60 side)

图 58/Figure 58

图 59/Figure 59

图 60 正面 /Figure 60 front

图 60 侧面 /Figure 60 side

动作十七：同动作八，唯左右相反。（图 61 正面、图 61 背面）

Movement 17: Repeat Movement 8, but only with left and right reversed. (Figure 61 front, Figure 61 back)

动作十八：同动作九，唯左右相反。（图 62）

Movement 18: Repeat Movement 9, but only with left and right reversed. (Figure 62)

动作十九：同动作十，唯左右相反。（图 63）

Movement 19: Repeat Movement 10, but only with left and right reversed. (Figure 63)

图 61 正面 /Figure 61 front

图 61 背面 /Figure 61 back

图 62/Figure 62

图 63/Figure 63

重复动作二至动作十七；左右动作为一遍，共做两遍，接做动作二十。

Repeat Movements 2 to 17. The movements on the left once and the movements on the right once form a routine. Do the routine twice, followed by Movement 20.

动作二十：两腿自然站立；同时，两拳变掌，分别经左右两侧向头顶上方环抱，指尖相对，配合吸气；目视前方。（图 64）

Movement 20: Straighten your legs naturally. At the same time, opening into palms, your hands move upward from the sides of the body respectively, fingers pointing to each other over your head. Inhale. Eyes look ahead. (Figure 64)

动作二十一：沉肩垂肘，两臂内收，两手至胸前十指相对，继续下按与肚脐同高，掌心向下，两手指尖相距约 10 厘米；两掌距肚脐约 10 厘米；同时，屈膝下蹲，大小腿夹角约 45°；配合呼气；目视前下方。（图 65）

Movement 21: With your shoulders sinking and elbows dropping, press your hands down to your chest, palms down, fingers pointing to each other, and further down to your navel height, about 10cm apart. The palms are about 10cm away from the navel. At the same time, bend your knees at about 45°. Exhale. Eyes look down to the front. (Figure 65)

图 64/Figure 64

图 65/Figure 65

二、学练要领

II. Key Points

1. 两臂下落时，沉肩垂肘，节节放松。

When your arms fall, sink your shoulders and elbows, and relax joints one by one .

2. 两臂同时上举时腰部要放松牵引，两手由拳变掌经两侧下落时，要松肩、坠肘、引腕，用合谷穴轻敲大腿外侧胆经。

When raising your arms, relax and extend your waist. When your palms drop down from both sides, relax your shoulders, drop your elbows and extend your wrists, tapping the gallbladder meridians on the outer thighs with *Hegu* acupoints.

3. 左右转身抡臂时，立身中正，以腰带臂。

When swinging your arms to the left and right, stand upright with your waist as the driving force.

4. 动作八松髋松腰下蹲，借助手臂下落的惯性，两拳轻敲下腹部的气海穴和骶骨，前后敲击要同步进行。

In Movement 8, as your knees bend slightly, with the momentum of falling arms, tap *Qihai* acupoint and the sacrum with two fists simultaneously.

5. 整个动作过程，柔和缓慢速度均匀，意识引导内力不断。

The movements should be gentle, slow and even, with intention guiding the internal force constantly.

三、功理功用

III. Functions and Effects

1. 脊柱左右旋转，可增强腰部的灵活性。

Rotate your spine left or right to enhance the flexibility of the waist.

2. 敲击胆经和震荡丹田，鼓荡正气，培补元气，提高抗病能力。

Tap the gallbladder meridians and shake the *Dantian* to swell *Qi* like a drum, invigorating premordial energy, so that you can increase your ability to resist illness.

3. 通过躯干四肢放松下落的惯性和自身重力作用的被动牵引，使髋膝踝等均得到牵拉，对下肢关节有良好的保健作用。

Through the inertia of the torso and limbs falling down under the action of the body's own weight, the hips, knees and ankles can be pulled, which has a good health effect on the joints of lower limbs.

四、适宜症状

IV. Indications

1. 可以缓解腰膝酸软无力，平衡感差，肢体不协调等症状。

It can relieve soreness and weakness of waist and knees, poor sense of balance, and body-limb incoordination.

2. 可缓解各种疼痛症状。

It can relieve various pains.

3. 改善失眠、多梦等症状。

It can improve insomnia and dreaminess.

第五式　揉脊势

Posture 5　Rub Spine

一、功法操作

I. Instructions

动作一：重心左移收右脚成右丁步；同时，左臂向下、向左、向上划弧摆至左侧侧平举，掌心向下，右臂摆至腋下与大包穴同高，掌心向下，指尖向左；配合吸气；目视左手。（图 66）

图 66/Figure 66

Movement 1: With the weight shifting to the left, bring your right foot close to the left into a T-shaped stance. At the same time, move your left arm downward, leftward and upward in an arc to shoulder height, palm downward, and your right arm under the left armpit at the same height as *Dabao* acupoint, palm down, fingers pointing to the left. Inhale. Eyes look at your left hand. (Figure 66)

动作二：动作不停，左腿保持屈膝约 45°，右脚以脚掌为轴外旋至脚尖向右，同时，臀向左摆，躯干右倾至垂线向右约 45°，带动左臂向上、向右摆至右斜上方约 45°，掌心向上，指尖向右；右手在距大包穴约 10 厘米处，在身体左侧立掌外推，掌心向左，指尖向上；目随左手环视，先看头上方，后向右转头，视右斜下方；配合呼气，动作略停。（图 67 正面、图 67 背面）

Movement 2: Without a pause, keep your left leg bent at about 45°. With the ball of foot pivoting, turn your right foot outward until the toes point to the right. At the same time, with your hips swinging to the left, lean your torso about 45° to the right from the vertical line, driving your left arm up to the right at about 45° from the vertical line, palm up, fingers pointing to the right. Your right hand is about 10cm away from *Dabao* acupoint, pushing outward with the palm on the left side of the body, facing the left, fingers pointing up. Eyes look around with your left hand, first above your head, and then obliquely down to the right, as your head turns to the right. Exhale. Make a short pause. (Figure 67 front, Figure 67 back)

图 67 正面 /Figure 67 front

图 67 背面 /Figure 67 back

动作三：左腿动作保持不变，右脚以脚掌为轴内旋至脚尖向前，身体还原至中正状态；左臂向上、向左摆至侧平举，右手掌心向下，指尖向左；目随左手环视，先看头上方，后向左转头，目视身体左侧。（图 68）

Movement 3: With the position of your left leg unchanged, turn your right foot inward around the ball of the foot until the toes point forward. Your body returns to the upright position. Swing your left arm up and left to shoulder height, with your right palm down, fingers pointing to the left. Eyes look around with your left hand, first above your head, and then to the left as your head turns to the left. (Figure 68)

动作四：右脚向右开步，略宽于肩，重心右移收左脚成左丁步；同时两臂向下、向右、向上划弧摆动，右臂摆至侧平举，掌心向下，左臂摆至腋下与大包穴同高，掌心向下，指尖向右；配合吸气；目视右手。（图 69）

Movement 4: Step to the right with your right foot, slightly wider than your shoulder width. With your weight shifting to the right, bring your left foot close to the right into a T-shaped stance. At the same time, swing your arms downwards, rightwards and upwards in an arc, with the right one at shoulder height, palm down, and the left one under the right armpit at the same height as *Dabao* acupoint, palm down, fingers pointing right. Inhale. Eyes look at your right hand. (Figure 69)

图 68/Figure 68

图 69/Figure 69

动作五：同动作二，唯左右相反。（图 70 正面、图 70 背面）

Movement 5: Repeat Movement 2, but only with left and right reversed. (Figure 70 front, Figure 70 back)

动作六：同动作三，唯左右相反。（图 71）

Movement 6: Repeat Movement 3, but only with left and right reversed. (Figure 71)

图 70 正面 /Figure 70 front

图 70 背面 /Figure 70 back

图 71/Figure 71

重复动作二至动作六一遍；本式动作一左一右为一遍，共做两遍；接做动作七。

Repeat Movements 2 to 6. The movements on the left once and the movements on the right once form a routine. Do the routine twice, followed by Movement 7.

动作七：左脚开步，稍宽于肩，自然站立，两脚尖向前；同时左臂从下向上侧平举，右臂自然伸展成侧平举，掌心向上；目视前方。（图 72）

Movement 7: Step to the left with your left foot, slightly wider than shoulder width. Stand naturally, toes pointing forward. At the same time, swing your left arm downward and upward to shoulder height. Extend your right arm horizontally to shoulder height, palm up. Eyes look ahead. (Figure 72)

动作八：两手上抱指尖相对；配合吸气；目视前方。（图 73）

Movement 8: Raise your hands up, fingers pointing to each other. Inhale. Eyes look ahead. (Figure 73)

图 72/Figure 72

图 73/Figure 73

动作九：沉肩垂肘两臂内收，两手至胸前十指相对，继续下按与肚脐同高，掌心向下，两手指尖相距约 10 厘米；两掌距肚脐约 10 厘米；同时，屈膝下蹲，大小腿夹角约 45°；配合呼气；目视前下方。（图 74）

图 74/Figure 74

Movement 9: With your shoulders sinking and elbows dropping, press your hands down to your chest, palms down, fingers pointing to each other, and further down to your navel height, about 10cm apart. The palms are about 10cm away from the navel. At the same time, bend your knees at about 45°. Exhale. Eyes look down to the front. (Figure 74)

二、学练要领

II. Key Points

1. 身体左倾或右倾时，手臂放松伸展，以腰带臂，过渡动作慢不停，从下向上节节贯穿，上下相随，充分侧拉。

When your torso leans to the left or right, relax and extend your arms, with the waist as the driving force. The transitional moves go slowly and continuously from joint to joint, to stretch sideways fully.

2. 左脚或右脚以脚掌为轴外展或内旋时，要踝磨涌泉穴。

When your left or right foot turns outward or inward around the ball of foot, grind *Yongquan* acupoint.

3. 动作配合呼吸，起吸落呼，动作柔缓、飘逸。

Coordinate your movements with breathing, rising with inhaling and falling with exhaling. Make your movements as soft and flowing as possible.

三、功理功用

III. Functions and Effects

1. 脊柱左右伸展与侧屈，增强脊柱关节周围韧带的伸展性、弹性和肌肉力量，维护关节的稳定性。预防和调整脊柱生理弯曲、不对称、不平衡等现象，有效地避免脊柱在形态上的不良变化。

Lateral leaning and extension of the spine can enhance the extensibility, elasticity of ligaments and the strength of muscle around the spine, maintaining the stability of the joints, and preventing and adjusting the physiological bending, asymmetry and imbalance of the spine, so as to avoid the adverse changes in the shape of the spine.

2. 身体侧屈和腿外旋可以有效刺激胆经、冲脉和任督二脉等重要经脉，有助于疏肝利胆，宣发肺气，促进全身气血运行。

Lateral leaning and outward rotation of legs can effectively stimulate gallbladder, *Chong*, *Ren* and *Du* meridians, which is helpful to soothe liver-gallbladder, and ventilate the lung *Qi*, promoting *Qi* and blood circulation in the whole body.

四、适宜症状

IV. Indications

可以缓解肝胆脏腑疾病、脾胃消化不良、泌尿系统疾病、颈椎病、腰肌劳损、脊柱侧弯、椎间盘突出等症状。

It can relieve liver and gallbladder diseases, spleen and stomach dyspepsia, urinary system diseases, cervical spondylosis, lumbar muscle strain, scoliosis, and intervertebral disc herniation.

第六式　摆臀势

Posture 6　Swing Hips

一、功法操作

I. Instructions

动作一：接上式动作，下颌内收，低头含胸，颈椎、胸椎、腰椎、骶椎、尾椎从上向下逐节卷曲；同时，两掌下落至两膝之间；掌背相靠，指尖向下；目视两掌。（图 75）

图 75/Figure 75

Movement 1: Continuing from the end of the previous posture, with the lower jaw and chest tucked in, lower your head, bending the cervical, thoracic, lumbar, sacral and caudal vertebrae from top to bottom, one by one. At the same time, drop your palms down to between your knees, back to back, fingers pointing down. Eyes look at your palms. (Figure 75)

动作二：从尾椎至颈椎逐节伸展成自然站立；同时提肘至两前臂水平，掌背相靠，指尖向下；目视前方。（图 76）

Movement 2: Stretching from caudal vertebra to cervical vertebra one by one, straighten your legs to stand naturally. At the same time, raise your elbows to the level of your forearms, with the backs of your palms against each other, fingers pointing down. Eyes look ahead. (Figure 76)

动作三：松髋屈膝下蹲，两腿屈膝约 45°；同时，松肩坠肘胸前合掌，掌心涵空；目视前下方。（图 77）

Movement 3: Loosen your hips and bend your knees at about 45°. At the same time, with your shoulders relaxed and your elbows sinking, hold the palms together in front of the chest, hollowed in between. Look down to the front. (Figure 77)

图 76/Figure 76

图 77/Figure 77

动作四：保持立身中正，臀部向左斜前方缓缓摆动；同时，两掌向左斜前方缓缓推出，两臂撑圆；配合呼气；动作略停，目视左前下方。（图 78 正面、图 78 背面）

Movement 4: With your upper body upright, swing your hips slowly to the left and diagonally forward. At the same time, push your joined palms slowly to the left and diagonally forward, arms rounded. Exhale. Make a short pause. Eyes look down at the left front. (Figure 78 front, Figure 78 back)

动作五：臀、臂还原至中正，同动作三。（图 79）

Movement 5: Bring your hips and arms back to the original positions. Repeat Movement 3. (Figure 79)

动作六：同动作四，唯左右相反。（图 80 正面、图 80 背面）

Movement 6: Repeat Movement 4, but only with left and right reversed. (Figure 80 front, Figure 80 back)

动作七：臀、臂还原至中正，同动作三。（图 81）

Movement 7: Bring your hips and arms back to the original positions. Repeat Movement 3. (Figure 81)

图 78 正面 /Figure 78 front

图 78 背面 /Figure 78 back

图 79/Figure 79

图 80 正面 /Figure 80 front

图 80 背面 /Figure 80 back

图 81/Figure 81

重复动作四至动作七 1 遍，接做动作八。

Repeat Movements 4 to 7 once, followed by Movement 8.

动作八：两脚、两膝和头的动作保持不变，向左摆臀，同时，两手合掌以腕为轴，指尖向左倾斜约 45°；动作不停，尾椎向顺时针方向转平圆两圈；目随两掌环视。（图 82 正面、图 82 背面）

Movement 8: With the positions of your head, knees and feet

unchanged, swing your hips to the left. At the same time, with the wrists of your joined palms pivoting, tilt your fingers to the left at about 45°. Without a pause, turn your tailbone clockwise in a flat circle twice. Eyes look around with your joined palms. (Figure 82 front, Figure 82 back)

图 82 正面 /Figure 82 front

图 82 背面 /Figure 82 back

动作九：两腿屈膝下蹲约 45°，脚尖向前；立身中正；两手合掌于胸前，掌心涵空；目视前下方。（图 83）

Movement 9: Bend your knees at about 45°, toes pointing forward. Keep your upper body upright. Hold your hands together in front of your chest, hollowed in between. Eyes look down to the front. (Figure 83)

图 83/Figure 83

动作十：同动作八，唯左右相反，尾椎和两掌同时向逆时针方向转平圆两圈。（图 84 正面、图 84 背面）

Movement 10: Repeat Movement 8, but only with left and right reversed. Turn your tail bone and joined palms anticlockwise in a flat circle twice. (Figure 84 front, Figure 84 back)

图 84 正面 /Figure 84 front

图 84 背面 /Figure 84 back

动作十一：同动作九。（图 85）

Movement 11: Repeat Movement 9. (Figure 85)

动作十二：头、躯干、腿部动作保持不变；两掌外旋掌心向上，两小指靠拢，指尖向前；目视两掌。（图 86）

Movement 12: With the positions of your head, torso and legs unchanged, turn your palms outward, facing up, with your little fingers together, pointing forward. Eyes look at palms. (Figure 86)

图 85/Figure 85

图 86/Figure 86

动作十三：头、躯干、腿部动作保持不变；掌心向上，两手腕内旋，指尖从腋下反穿至肩胛骨下，手腕轻贴于脊柱两侧，掌心向后，指尖向下；目视前方。（图 87 正面、图 87 背面）

Movement 13: Keep the positions of your head, torso and legs unchanged. With your palms facing up, turn your wrists inward, fingers piercing back from the armpits to below the shoulder blades so that your wrists are lightly attached to the sides of the spine, palms backward, and fingers pointing downward. Eyes look ahead. (Figure 87 front, Figure 87 back)

图 87 正面 /Figure 87 front

图 87 背面 /Figure 87 back

动作十四：缓缓起身，两腿自然站立；同时，两掌掌背下推按摩至环跳穴；目视前方。（图 88 正面、图 88 背面）

Movement 14: Straighten your legs slowly and stand naturally. At the same time, massage with the backs of your palms downward to *Huantiao* acupoints. Eyes look ahead. (Figure 88 front, Figure 88 back)

动作十五：头、躯干、腿部动作保持不变；两臂缓缓外旋侧起至侧平举；目视前方。（图 89）

Movement 15: With the positions of your head, torso and legs unchanged, rotate your arms outward slowly, raising them from the sides of your body to shoulder height. Eyes look ahead. (Figure 89)

动作十六：两掌向上环抱，指尖相对；配合吸气；目视前方。（图 90）

Movement 16: Raise your hands upward, fingers pointing to each other over your head. Inhale. Eyes look ahead. (Figure 90)

图 88 正面 /Figure 88 front

图 88 背面 /Figure 88 back

图 89/Figure 89

图 90/Figure 90

动作十七：沉肩垂肘两臂内收，两手至胸前十指相对，继续下按与肚脐同高，掌心向下，两手指尖相距约 10 厘米；两掌距肚脐约 10 厘米；同时，屈膝下蹲，大小腿夹角约45°；配合呼气；目视前下方。（图 91）

图 91/Figure 91

Movement 17: With your shoulders sinking and elbows dropping, press your hands down to your chest, palms down, fingers pointing to each other, and further down to your navel height, about 10cm apart. The palms are about 10cm away from the navel. At the same time, bend your knees at about 45°. Exhale. Eyes look down to the front. (Figure 91)

二、学练要领

II. Key Points

1. 从掌背相靠到掌心相合，要配合脊柱的卷曲和伸展，节节贯穿，柔和连贯。

The movements of palms from “back to back” to “palm to palm” should cooperate with the soft flexion and extension of the spine, joint by joint.

2. 摆臀时，以尾椎为着力点，腰椎、胸椎顺势摆动，速度均匀，重心不变。

When swinging hips, use your tail bone to drive the lumbar vertebra and thoracic vertebra to swing with a uniform speed and constant weight.

3. 手尾旋转方向一致，动作幅度不宜过大。

Turn your hands and tail bone in the same direction, with moderate movement range.

三、功理功用

III. Functions and Effects

1. 摆臀动作，以尾椎带动身体的运动，可以按摩脊柱和内脏，增强腰、髋关节的稳定性。

Hip swinging, which drives the movement of the body by the tail bone, can massage the spine and internal organs to enhance the stability of the waist and hip joints.

2. 合掌旋转，对肩、肘、腕起到了按摩和牵拉的作用。

Turning with the joined palms can massage and pull the shoulders, elbows and wrists.

3. 调理任脉、督脉和带脉，对腰腿劳损有保健康复作用。

The regulation of *Ren*, *Du* and belt meridians helps relieve waist and leg strains.

四、适宜症状

IV. Indications

可改善心胸憋闷，心律不齐，四肢冰冷，腰肌劳损，消化系统紊乱等症状。

It can improve chest congestion, arrhythmia, cold limbs, lumbar muscle strain and digestive system disorder.

第七式　摩肋势

Posture 7　Massage Ribs

一、功法操作

I. Instructions

动作一：接上式动作，两腿自然站立；同时两臂侧平举，掌心向下；配合吸气，目视前方。（图 92）

Movement 1: Continuing from the end of the previous posture, straighten your legs and stand naturally. At the same time, raise your arms to shoulder height and extend them horizontally, palms down. Inhale. Eyes look ahead. (Figure 92)

动作二：左脚内扣约 45°，膝微屈；身体右转，右脚以脚跟为轴外展约 90°，勾脚尖；同时，抡臂转身，左臂向上，掌心向前，

图 92/Figure 92

图 93/Figure 93

指尖向上，右臂向下，掌心向后，指尖向下。（图 93）

Movement 2: Turn your left foot inward at about 45°, knee slightly bent. With your body turning right, turn your right foot outward at about 90° around the heel, toes up. At the same time, swing your left arm up, palm forward, fingertips pointing up, and right arm down, palm back, fingers pointing down. (Figure 93)

动作三：动作不停，身体前俯；左腿屈膝，右腿自然伸展；左臂向下至左掌心轻贴右脚尖，指尖向前；右臂伸展向后摆至斜上方，掌心向前，指尖向后斜上方；目视前下方。（图 94 正面、图 94 背面）

Movement 3: Without a pause, lean forward, left leg bent, right leg naturally straight. Move your left arm downward until the left palm lightly touches the right toes, fingers pointing forward; and extend your right arm and swing it backward and obliquely upward, palm forward, fingers pointing obliquely up. Eyes look down at the front. (Figure 94 front, Figure 94 back)

图 94 正面 /Figure 94 front

图 94 背面 /Figure 94 back

动作四：右掌收至右腋下，掌心向内，指尖斜向下。（图 95）

Movement 4: Bring your right palm to the right armpit, palm inward, fingers pointing obliquely downward. (Figure 95)

动作五：右脚向右后方退步成左虚步，同时，缓缓起身，随之向左转腰；右掌根沿腋下中线推摩至髋关节下方后，继续上摆至前平举，掌心向下，指尖向前；左掌经左髋外侧掌根轻贴身体上提至腋下，掌心向内，指尖向斜下；配合呼气；目视右手。（图 96）

Movement 5: Step back to the right with your right foot into a right-weighted empty stance. At the same time, rise slowly, turning your waist to the left. After rubbing the base of the right palm downward along the sideline of the torso to the lower part of the hip, swing your right palm up to the front and extend it horizontally, facing down, fingers pointing forward. Lift your left palm to the armpit, facing inward the base of palm touching the rib, fingers pointing obliquely downward. Exhale. Eyes look at your right hand. (Figure 96)

图 95/Figure 95

图 96/Figure 96

动作六：同动作五，唯左右相反。（图 97）

Movement 6: Repeat Movement 5, but only with left and right reversed. (Figure 97)

动作七：同动作五。（图 98）

Movement 7: Repeat Movement 5. (Figure 98)

动作八：左脚向左后方退步成右虚步。同时，缓缓起身，随之向右转腰；左掌根沿腋下中线推摩至髋关节下方后，继续上摆至前平举，掌心向下，指尖向前；右掌从体前向下弧形摆至身体右后方，掌心向后，指尖向斜下方；配合呼气，目视左手。（图 99）

图 97/Figure 97

图 98/Figure 98

Movement 8: Step back to the left with your left foot into a right-weighted empty stance. At the same time, rise slowly, turning your waist to the right. After rubbing the base of the left palm downward along the sideline of the torso to the lower part of the hip, swing your left palm up to the front and extend horizontally, facing down, fingers pointing forward. Swing your right palm downward in an arc from the front of the body to the right rear, facing backward, fingers pointing obliquely downward. Exhale. Eyes look at your left hand. (Figure 99)

图 99/Figure 99

共退 4 步，一右一左为一遍，做两遍摩肋后，接做动作九。

Take 4 steps back in all. The movements on the left once and the movements on the right once form a routine. Rub your ribs twice, followed by Movement 9.

动作九：左腿屈膝，右腿自然伸展，脚尖勾起；同时，身体前俯，左掌下按掌心贴右脚尖，指尖向前；右臂伸展向后摆至斜上方，掌心向前，指尖向后上方；配合呼气；目视前下方。（图 100）

图 100/Figure 100

Movement 9: With your left leg bent, straighten your right leg naturally, toes up. At the same time, with your body leaning forward, press your left palm downward to touch the right toes, fingers pointing forward; and extend your right arm and swing it backward and obliquely upward, palm forward, fingers pointing obliquely up. Exhale. Eyes look down at the front. (Figure 100)

动作十：起身，右脚掌内扣约 135°，左脚以脚跟为轴外展约 135°，勾脚尖；同时，身体左转约 180°；抡臂转身，左臂内旋从前、向上、经头顶弧线向下、向后，掌心向后，指尖向斜下方，右臂外旋向下，从右向上至头顶，掌心向前，指尖向上。（图 101、图 102）

图 101/Figure 101

图 102/Figure 102

Movement 10: Rise up, with your right foot turning about 135° inward and your left foot turning about 135° outward around the heel, toes up. At the same time, with the body turning about 180° to the left, swing your inward-rotating left arm forward, upward, past the head, downward, and backward, palm backward, fingers pointing obliquely downward, and your outward-rotating right arm downward, and upward from the right to above your head, palm forward, fingers pointing up. (Figure 101, Figure 102)

动作十一：动作不停，身体前俯；右腿屈膝，左腿自然伸展，脚尖勾起；右臂向下至右掌心轻贴左脚尖，指尖向前；左臂伸展向后摆至斜上方，掌心向前，指尖向后斜上方；配合呼气；目视前下方。（图 103）

图 103/Figure 103

Movement 11: Without a pause, lean forward. With your right leg bent, straighten your left leg naturally, toes up. Press your right arm downward to touch the left toes with your right palm, fingers pointing forward; and extend your left arm and swing it backward and obliquely upward, palm forward, fingers pointing obliquely up. Exhale. Eyes look down at the front. (Figure 103)

动作十二：同动作四，唯左右相反。（图 104 正面、图 104 背面）

Movement 12: Repeat Movement 4, but only with left and right reversed. (Figure 104 front, Figure 104 back)

动作十三：同动作五，唯左右相反。（图 105）

Movement 13: Repeat Movement 5, but only with left and right reversed. (Figure 105)

动作十四：同动作五。（图 98）

Movement 14: Repeat Movement 5. (Figure 98)

图 104 正面 /Figure 104 front

图 104 背面 /Figure 104 back

共退 4 步，一左一右为一遍，做两遍摩肋后，接做动作十五。

Take 4 steps back in all. The movements on the left once and the movements on the right once form a routine. Rub your ribs twice, followed by Movement 15.

动作十五：同动作五，唯左右相反。（图 105）

Movement 15: Repeat Movement 5, but only with left and right reversed. (Figure 105)

动作十六：同动作八，唯左右相反。（图 106）

Movement 16: Repeat Movement 8, but only with left and right reversed. (Figure 106)

图 105/Figure 105

图 106/Figure 106

动作十七：同动作九，唯左右相反。（图 107）

Movement 17: Repeat Movement 9, but only with left and right reversed. (Figure 107)

动作十八：起身右转约 90°；左脚掌内扣约 90°，右脚尖外展约 45°，两脚尖平行向前，约与肩宽，自然站立；以腰带臂，右臂内旋从前、向上，经头顶弧线向下至侧平举，左臂外旋向下，从左向上摆至侧平举。（图 108）

Movement 18: Rise up, turning about 90° to the right . Turn your left foot about 90° inward around the heel, and your right foot about 45° outward around the heel, to straighten your legs naturally at shoulder-width, toes pointing forward. With the waist as the driving force, turn your right arm inward, forward, upward, past the head, and downward to extend it horizontally at shoulder height, and turn your left arm outward, downward, and upward from the left to extend it horizontally at shoulder height. (Figure 108)

图 107/Figure 107

图 108/Figure 108

动作十九：两掌向上环抱，指尖相对；配合吸气；目视前方。（图 109）

Movement 19: Raise your hands upward, fingers pointing to each other over your head. Inhale. Eyes look ahead. (Figure 109)

动作二十：沉肩垂肘两臂内收，两手至胸前十指相对，继续下按与肚脐同高，掌心向下，两手指尖相距约 10 厘米；两掌距肚脐约 10 厘米；同时，屈膝下蹲，大小腿夹角约 45°；配合呼气；目视前下方。（图 110）

Movement 20: With your shoulders sinking and elbows dropping, press your hands down to your chest, palms down, fingers pointing to each other, and further down to your navel height, about 10cm apart. The palms are about 10cm away from the navel. At the same time, bend your knees at about 45°. Exhale. Eyes look down to the front. (Figure 110)

图 109/Figure 109

图 110/Figure 110

二、学练要领

II. Key Points

1. 左右转腰摩肋，以腰带臂，牵引两胁肋部左旋右转。

As you turn your waist left or right and rub your rib, use your waist to drive the arms, pulling the two ribs to turn left or right.

2. 掌根从大包穴开始向下摩运，幅度要尽可能加大，推摩要顺达。

Starting from *Dabao* acupoint, rub down the sideline of the body with the base of hand smoothly and as long as possible.

3. 左右转身抡臂时，充分抻拉两胁肋部，以腰带臂，节节伸展。

When turning left or right to swing your arms, fully stretch your ribs. Use your waist to drive the arms, joint by joint.

三、功理功用
III. Functions and Effects

1. 通过抡臂可增强肩关节的灵活性，俯身攀足和腿的屈伸，可增强下肢柔韧性。

Swinging arms can help enhance the flexibility of shoulder joints, and bending over to touch your feet can enhance the flexibility of lower limbs.

2. 通过脊柱的左右旋转，两手摩运两胁肋部和大包穴，可起到疏肝和脾，强肾壮腰的作用。

Rotating the spine to the left or right and rubbing the rib and *Dabao* acupoint with your hand can help soothe the liver, activate the spleen, and strengthen the kidney and waist.

四、适宜症状
IV. Indications

缓解肝胆脏腑疾病，脾胃消化不良，泌尿系统疾病等症状。

It can relieve liver and gallbladder diseases, spleen and stomach dyspepsia, and urinary system diseases.

第八式　飞身势

Posture 8　Flying Stance

一、功法操作

I. Instructions

动作一：右腿自然伸展独立站立，左腿屈膝提起，脚尖自然下垂；同时，两臂分别向左右两侧斜后方摆起至左右两侧斜上方，肘微屈，掌心向下；配合吸气；目视前方。（图 111）

图 111/Figure 111

Movement 1: Straighten your right leg naturally and stand on it, with the left knee lifted, toes drooping. At the same time, raise your arms obliquely back to the left and right, pausing above shoulder level, elbows slightly bent, palms facing downward. Inhale. Eyes look ahead. (Figure 111)

动作二：右腿屈膝，左脚向左前约 30° 上步，脚尖向前；两臂分别向前下方划弧下落至身体两侧，两掌约与肚脐同高，掌心向下，指尖分别向左右斜前方；配合呼气；目视前下方。（图 112）

Movement 2: With your right leg bent, step forward to the left at about 30° with your left foot, toes pointing forward. Arc your arms down and forward to both sides of the body, at navel level, palms facing down, fingers pointing forward to the left and right respectively. Exhale. Eyes look to the lower front. (Figure 112)

动作三：左腿自然伸展独立站立，右腿屈膝提起，脚尖自然下垂；同时，两臂分别向左右两侧斜后方摆起至左右两侧斜上方，肘微屈，掌心向下；配合吸气；目视前方。（图 113）

Movement 3: Straighten your left leg naturally and stand on it, with the right knee lifted, toes drooping. At the same time, raise your arms obliquely back to the left and right, pausing above shoulder level, elbows slightly bent, palms facing downward. Inhale. Eyes look ahead. (Figure 113)

图 112/Figure 112

图 113/Figure 113

动作四：左腿屈膝，右脚向右前约 30° 上步，脚尖向前；两臂分别向前下方划弧下落至身体两侧，两掌约与肚脐同高，掌心向下，指尖分别向左右斜前方；配合呼气；目视前下方。（图 114）

Movement 4: With your left leg bent, step forward to the right at about 30° with your right foot, toes pointing forward. Arc your arms down and forward to both sides of the body, at navel level, palms facing down, fingers pointing forward to the left and right respectively. Exhale. Eyes look to the lower front. (Figure 114)

动作五：同动作一。

Movement 5: Repeat Movement 1.

动作六：同动作二。

Movement 6: Repeat Movement 2.

动作七：同动作三。（图 115）

Movement 7: Repeat Movement 3. (Figure 115)

图 114/Figure 114

图 115/Figure 115

动作八：右脚下落于左脚内侧成并步，屈膝下蹲，大小腿夹角约 45°；同时，两臂分别向前下方划弧下落至身体两侧，两掌约与肚脐同高，掌心向下，指尖分别向左右斜前方；配合呼气；目视前下方。（图 116）

Movement 8: Bring your right foot down on the inner side of your left foot, knees bent, with the angle between the thigh and the calf about 45°. At the same time, arc your arms forward and downward to the sides of the body, palms about the same height as the navel, facing downward, fingers pointing forward to the left and right respectively; Exhale. Eyes look to the lower front. (Figure 116)

动作一至动作八向前共上 4 步。

Make 4 steps forward from Movement 1 to Movement 8.

动作九：两腿缓缓伸展，膝微屈，头和躯干向右后方纵轴旋转，左臂外旋上举，上臂向斜上，掌心向外，指尖向前上方，右

臂内旋后摆至斜后方，掌心向外，指尖向后下方；配合呼气；动作略停，目视右下方。（图 117）

Movement 9: Straighten your legs slowly, knees slightly bent. Rotate your head and torso to the right and back around the spine. Lift your outward-rotating left arm, upper arm obliquely up, palm out, fingers pointing forward and up; swing your inward-rotating right arm back to the oblique rear, palm out, fingers pointing back and down. Exhale. Make a short pause. Eyes look down to the right. (Figure 117)

图 116/Figure 116

图 117/Figure 117

动作十：两腿缓缓伸直站立，身体还原至中正，同时肩、髋放松，以腰带臂，左臂内旋下落，右臂外旋上摆，至两臂成侧平举，掌心向下，指尖向左右两侧；配合吸气；目视前方。（图 118）

Movement 10: Straighten your legs slowly, and return your body to the original upright position. At the same time, relax your shoulders and hips. With your waist driving, drop your inward-rotating left arm down and swing your outward-rotating right arm up until they extend horizontally at shoulder level, palms down, fingers pointing to the left and right respectively. Inhale. Eyes look ahead. (Figure 118)

动作十一：两腿屈膝下蹲，大小腿夹角约 45°；同时，两臂分别向前下方下落至身体两侧，两掌约与肚脐同高，掌心向下，指尖分别向左右斜前方；配合呼气；目视前下方。（图 119）

Movement 11: Bend your knees with the angle between the thigh and the calf about 45°. At the same time, arc your arms forward and downward to the sides of the body, palms about the same height as the navel, facing downward, fingers pointing forward to the left and right respectively. Exhale. Eyes look to the lower front. (Figure 119)

图 118/Figure 118

图 119/Figure 119

动作十二：同动作三。（图 120）

Movement 12: Repeat Movement 3. (Figure 120)

动作十三：左腿屈膝，右脚向右后方约 30°退步，脚尖斜向前方；同时，两臂分别向前下方划弧下落至身体两侧，两掌约与肚脐同高，掌心向下，指尖分别向左右斜前方；配合呼气；目视前下方。（图 121）

Movement 13: Bend your left leg and step backwards with your right foot by about 30° to the right, toes pointing obliquely forward. At the same time, arc your arms forward and downward to the sides of the body, palms about the same height as the navel, facing downward, fingers pointing forward to the left and right respectively. Exhale. Eyes look to the lower front. (Figure 121)

图 120/Figure 120

图 121/Figure 121

动作十四：同动作一。（图 122）

Movement 14: Repeat Movement 1 (Figure 122).

动作十五：右腿屈膝，左脚向左后约 30° 退步，脚尖向斜前方；同时，两臂分别向前下方划弧下落至身体两侧，两掌约与肚脐同高，掌心向下，指尖分别向左右斜前方；配合呼气；目视前下方（图 123）。

Movement 15: Bend your right leg and step backwards with your left foot by about 30° to the left, toes pointing obliquely forward. At the same time, arc your arms forward and downward to the sides of the body, palms about the same height as the navel, facing downward, fingers pointing forward to the left and right respectively. Exhale. Eyes look to the lower front (Figure 123).

动作十六：同动作三。

Movement 16: Repeat Movement 3.

动作十七：同动作十三。

图 122/Figure 122

图 123/Figure 123

Movement 17: Repeat Movement 13.

动作十八：同动作一。

Movement 18: Repeat Movement 1.

动作十九：同动作八，唯左右脚相反。（图 124）

Movement 19: Repeat Movement 8, but bring your left foot down on the inner side of your right foot. (Figure 124)

图 124/Figure 124

动作十二至动作十九，共后退 4 步 。

Take 4 steps backward in all from Movement 12 till Movement 19.

动作二十：同动作九，唯左右相反。（图 125）

Movement 20: Repeat Movement 9, but only with left and right reversed. (Figure 125)

动作二十一：两腿缓缓伸直站立，身体还原至中正；同时肩、髋放松，以腰带臂，左臂内旋下落，右臂外旋上摆，至两臂成侧平举；掌心向上，指尖向左右两侧；配合吸气；目视前方。（图 126）

Movement 21: Straighten your legs slowly, and return your body to the original upright position. At the same time, relax your shoulders and hips. With your waist driving, drop your inward-rotating left arm down and swing your outward-rotating right arm up until they extend horizontally at shoulder level, palms up, fingers pointing to the left and right respectively. Inhale. Eyes look ahead. (Figure 126)

图 125/Figure 125

图 126/Figure 126

二、学练要领

II. Key Points

1. 上步或退步时，上下肢配合要协调，两臂向上摆动时提膝，两臂下落时落脚，重心要平稳，速度要均匀。

When stepping forward or backward, coordinate the upper and lower limbs. When swinging up the arms, lift your knee; when dropping them, land with your foot. The shift of weight should be smooth and the speed should be even.

2. 身体上升和下降时，脊柱有小幅度蠕动，节节贯穿，轻松自然。

When the body rises and falls, the spine moves slightly, joint by joint, in a relaxed and natural way.

3. 两脚并步站立，身体向右或向左旋转时，要根据自己的身体情况循序渐进，慢慢加大旋转幅度。

Stand with your feet together. When your body rotates to the right or left, you should slowly increase the rotation range little by little according to your physical condition.

4. 两臂上下旋转牵拉时，要对拔拉长，松紧适宜，协调配合。

When the rotating arms are pulled up and down, they should be stretched with appropriate tightness and coordination.

三、功理功用

III. Functions and Effects

通过两臂带动全身的气血升降，脊柱的蠕动和旋转，增加脊柱的稳定性，刺激中枢神经，摩运脏腑，通经活络。

The two arms drive the whole body's *Qi* and blood to rise and fall, and the spine to move and rotate, increasing the stability of the spine, stimulating the central nervous system, massaging the internal organs, and clearing and activating the channels and collaterals.

四、适宜症状

IV. Indications

可以提高肩颈和心肺功能，缓解颈椎病、腰肌劳损、少气无力、畏寒怕冷等症状。

It can improve the functions of shoulders and neck, heart and lungs, and relieve cervical spondylosis, lumbar muscle strain, hypodynamia, and chills.

收　势

Closing

一、功法操作

I. Instructions

动作一：两掌向上环抱，指尖相对；配合吸气；目视前方。（图127）

Movement 1: Raise your hands upward, fingers pointing to each other over your head. Inhale. Eyes look ahead. (Figure 127)

动作二：沉肩垂肘两臂内收，两掌下按与膈肌同高时，转掌心向内，继续下落与肚脐同高，两掌距肚脐约 10 厘米；配合呼气；目视前下方。（图 128）

Movement 2: With your shoulders sinking, elbows dropping and arms pulled inward, press your palms down to your diaphragm height.

图 127/Figure 127

图 128/Figure 128

Turning your palms inward, lower them further down to your navel height, about 10cm away. Exhale. Eyes look down to the front. (Figure 128)

重复动作一和动作二，共做三遍。接做动作三。

Repeat Movements 1 and 2 twice, followed by Movement 3.

动作三：两臂放松，自然下落，两掌中指轻贴腿外侧；自然呼吸，目视前方。（图 129）

Movement 3: Relax your arms and drop them naturally, middle fingers lightly on the outer thighs. Breathe naturally. Eyes look ahead. (Figure 129)

图 129/Figure 129

二、学练要领

II. Key Points

1. 手臂环抱，沉肩坠肘，引气归元，掌心对下丹田，停。

As you raise your hands upward, sink your shoulders, drop your elbows, and return *Qi* to its origin, palms to the abdomen. Make a short pause.

2. 动作松柔、自然流畅；心静体松，气定神敛。

Your movements should be soft, natural and flowing. Be calm and relaxed.

三、功理功用

III. Functions and Effects

收敛心神，引气归元。

Relax your mind and return *Qi* to its origin.

四、适宜症状

IV. Indications

缓解内心焦虑、精神紧张等症状。

It can relieve anxiety and mental stress.

大舞的呼吸要求

Breathing Requirements

首先遵循健身气功的基本呼吸方法是起吸落呼，开吸合呼；其次大舞的特殊要求是在做过渡动作时，呼吸要放慢但是不能停，细长均匀；在做定势动作时，呼吸要稍停。

First of all, adopt the basic breathing method of Health Qigong, that is, inhale as rising or opening and exhale as falling or closing. Secondly, the special requirement of Dawu is to breathe slowly and evenly when doing transitional movements, and make a pause in breathing in a fixed position.

学习建议

Learning Tips

1. 清楚动作的路线和方向。

Know clearly the route and direction of any movement.

2. 感悟动作的要求要领和呼吸方法。

Comprehend the requirements, essentials and breathing methods of any movement.

3. 了解和掌握动作所涉及到的脏腑、经络和穴位。

Understand and master the internal organs, meridians and acupoints involved in any movement.

4. 松贯始终，一点紧一片松，才能够更好地导引气血，使全身经脉畅通。

Be relaxed throughout. One tight spot alone with all the rest relaxed can help improve the circulation of *Qi* and blood and dredge the meridians.